HOW NOT TO WRITE A BOOK

12 Things You Should Never Do If You Want to Become an Author & Make a Living With Your Writing

(From Someone Who Has Written 12 Books in 12 Months)

MICHELLE KULP

Copyright © 2020 Michelle Kulp

Published by: Monarch Crown Publishing

ISBN: 978-1-7354188-5-8

TABLE OF CONTENTS

FREE GIFT FOR MY READERS:

1
AUTHOR
ARCHETYPE
ASSESSMENT

2
BOOK-A-MONTH
QUICKSTART KIT

3
FREE VIDEO
TRAINING FROM
MICHELLE KULP

I have a special gift for my readers! To help you on your writing journey, I have created a *Quick-Start Writing Kit* that includes:

- 16 Rapid Writing Secrets

- Bestseller Checklist

- Annual Publishing Chart

- Income Tracker

- Book Creation Outline Template

- Author Archetype Assessment

- Video Training

Sign up to receive your Quick-Start Kit at: https://BestsellingAuthorProgram.com/free-module-28-days-to-100k/

INTRODUCTION

Writers are troubled people.

Not only do we suffer from *writer's block*, but we also battle with intense and persistent *resistance* that is so powerful we will often do anything and everything… except sit down and write.

How many industries use the word "BLOCK" when talking about their trade or job title, as in **Writer's BLOCK?**

Why is writing so hard?
Why do 90% of people say they want to write a book,
but according to statistics, only 1% do?

Not very good odds if you ask me.

And why are there so many broke and struggling writers that there is a special term for them – **STARVING ARTISTS?**

Before I finally got the courage to sit down, fight through the resistance and my fears, and write my first book, I spent ten years:

- *Reading* about writing

- *Fantasizing* about the writer's life

- *Dreaming* of being a writer

- *Talking* to writers

- *Journaling* about writing

- *Attending* writers' conferences

It may seem crazy that I'm now writing a book about how *NOT* to write a book, but often when we learn what mistakes and pitfalls to AVOID, we can achieve our goals and dreams faster.

Let me give you a glimpse of my writing history:

- I spent over ten years doing everything except writing books.

- I tried for more than a year to get a publishing deal that never came through.

- I spent another year trying to get an agent.

- I decided to take matters into my own hands and self-published my first book on Amazon in 2011. I did everything wrong, no one could find my book, and I had ZERO sales.

- I spent another year figuring out what I did wrong and republished my next book in 2012, with the help of a book launch expert, and had much more success. I became a #1 bestselling author, and my book had 2,128 downloads in just one day.

- I didn't publish another book for three years.

- In 2015, I published two books

- In 2016, I published two books.

- In 2019, the income from my royalties for the entire year was $500.

As I look back on this list, I see that I wasted a lot of time, and I don't want you to do the same.

Sure, I published a few books here and there, but imagine what would have happened if I was consistently writing books during those 10+ years? I'd be making a lot of money right now and have dozens more books published.

Let me bring you up to the present time...

In 2013, I started my www.bestsellingauthorprogram.com helping authors write, publish and launch their books to the #1 bestsellers list through my done-for-you services.

That business turned into a multiple-six-figure business. To date, I've helped over 250 authors with their books.

Many of my clients have had great success and have created 6- and 7-figure businesses around them. I'm happy to say that I learn something new from every client's book. Knowledge is power.

After helping so many authors, I felt that I should be writing books, too. After all, writing is my passion.

It seemed *incongruous* that I was coaching and helping writers, but I wasn't writing books myself.

The truth was, I was living in the shadows.

At the end of 2019, I read an article on Written Word Media that said the average $100K author has 28 books in their catalog. I immediately thought, "I'm going to write a book a month and test this theory to see if I can make six figures with 28 books."

I'm not 100% sure where I came up with this crazy idea to write a book a month, but I went with it. Since January 2020, I've written and published a book a month. Yes. Every. Single. Month.

This book you're reading is the 12th consecutive book that I've published in 2020.

I'm happy to report that I've created $3,000 a month in passive income since I started on this book-a-month journey!

By the end of 2021, I should be close to hitting my goal of making six figures solely from my royalties!

My income now is significantly higher than the $500 I earned for all of 2019. In a few months, I'll be able to pay all of my living expenses with my royalties. Once my living expenses are covered, I can retire!

I detail my entire process and system in my bestselling book, *28 Books to $100K*. I also have a FREE Facebook group you can join if you're interested.

The purpose of this book is to teach you everything I know about how NOT to write a book, so you can avoid making these common mistakes and reach your writing goals and dreams.

I am an expert on NOT writing books because I didn't write for over a decade even though it was my dream. I found every distraction known to man to avoid sitting down and writing my book. I'm sure you can relate to what I'm saying, or you wouldn't be reading this book.

Not only do I have firsthand experience with NOT writing books, but many of my clients tell me, "I've been working on this book for (2/5/8/10 or more) years, and I can't seem to get it done."

The struggle is real.

I want to help writers get their books out of their heads and out to the world.

To achieve this, I've come up with the **12 Things You Should Never Do If You Want to Become an Author and Make a Living With Your Writing.**

Sometimes, we do things unconsciously that block our goals and desires. Unfortunately, we don't know what we're doing wrong, but essentially we are sabotaging ourselves because we are NOT getting the results we want.

This book will fix that.

By learning what NOT to do, you can have great success publishing your book(s) and also making a living with your writing.

If I can do it, you can too!

Let's get started…

CHAPTER 1
PAJAMA TIME

If you want to get your writing done, you absolutely must stay in your pajamas; or better yet, if you're alone, write naked (just kidding).

You must NOT, under any circumstances:

- Get dressed
- Talk on the phone
- Check your email
- Get on social media
- Run errands
- Clean
- Bake
- Read
- Shower
- Do laundry

I woke up five minutes ago, and right now, I'm sitting at my dining room table with my laptop, seven books that I plan to quote from, a cup of tea, and I'm writing.

I've been writing a book a month since January 2020, which means I have been battling resistance for 12 months.

Steven Pressfield, one of my favorite authors, says in his book, *The War of Art* and also *Going Pro*:

> *"Resistance stops us from committing to the important work of our lives—not just committing to it but fighting like hell to get it done."*

If you want to write a book, you should know that you have many battles ahead of you because there is a "perverse enemy" called *resistance* fighting against you.

You need to treat the *resistance* like the willful and powerful entity it is and know that it will show up every time you decide to sit down and work on your book.

The *resistance* doesn't want you to do your creative work. It wants to you to remain in the status quo.

Every time you commit to writing, the *resistance* will create sudden emergencies, difficulties, predicaments, problems, complications, and chaos that will prevent you from writing your book.

I find it incredibly ironic that the minute I decided to write a book a month, my 30-year-old daughter split up with her ex, and she and my two-year-old granddaughter came to live with me... for an entire year.

I found out that writing with a two-year-old in the house is next to impossible, or at least that's what I told myself. I was mentally, physically, and emotionally exhausted and seriously struggling to write a book a month. However, because I publicly announced that I was writing a book a month, I had to get it done, no matter what.

Because I've been an entrepreneur working on my own since 2005, I haven't had to wake up at a specific time. I wake up naturally when my body is well-rested.

Guess what?

With a two-year-old in my house, I was on high alert and not getting the amount of sleep I needed. So I did something totally against my nature; I set an alarm clock to get up before the little one did and get my writing done – **IN MY PAJAMAS**!

I found that no matter what good intentions I had, I wouldn't get my writing done that day if I did anything else first. *Anything* includes things like:

- My morning meditation
- My morning journaling
- My morning reading
- Running to Starbucks
- Going to the bank
- Cooking
- Responding to emails, texts or phone calls
- Getting on Social Media
- Cleaning
- Organizing
- Showering

Seriously, I would roll out of bed in my pajamas, open the computer, and start writing. That's the only thing that worked for me.

Even yesterday, for example, I had no client calls and nothing urgent to address, but somehow I managed NOT to write because I didn't follow my #1 rule – WRITE IN YOUR PAJAMAS!

By the way, I had every intention of spending the entire day writing. Here's what happened instead:

- I worked at the computer on a client's problem first thing in the morning which drained me

- I checked my email

- I checked social media

- I made a pot of homemade soup

- I made a smoothie

- I went to Starbucks

- I stopped by two stores looking for Christmas decorations for my daughter

- I went by my daughter and granddaughter's house to help them decorate the tree

- I answered several phone calls

By late afternoon, I had no energy to write.

I am serious when I say, the second you commit to writing, either you will come up with a million distractions or an emergency or crisis will show up to block your efforts.

If you're aware of this phenomenon, then you'll be better prepared to overcome it.

Another crisis that happened once I decided to write a book a month was…

COVID-19

It might not sound like a bad thing to be quarantined to your house when writing books. However, my 30-year-old daughter and two-year-old granddaughter were also quarantined in my house, in way too-close proximity. They were around me 24/7, and it wasn't easy to find a quiet place to write uninterrupted.

Many other things happened during the past 12 months that could have stopped me from writing my books, but that's a story for another time.

Once you are aware that this RESISTANCE wants to STOP you from writing, you have to find ways to outsmart the enemy.

In his book, *Turning Pro*, Steven Pressfield says this about NOT writing:

> *"Sitting down to do the work is another thing entirely.*
> *Call it writer's block, artistic agita, or general malaise,*
> *that malignant internal entity that keeps us from our*
> *calling can be a killer."*

He also says that when we turn Pro:

"...we give up a life with which we may have become extremely comfortable. We give up a self that we have come to identify and to call our own. We may have to give up friends, lovers, even spouses. Turning Pro is free, but it demands sacrifice. Turning Pro is not for everyone. We have to be a little crazy to do it or even to want to. In many ways the passage chooses us; we don't choose it. We simply have no alternative. What we get when we turn Pro is, we find our power. We find our will and our voice, and we find our self-respect. We become who we always were but had, until then, been afraid to embrace and to live out."

Every word of that statement is true.

I was an amateur for more than a decade, allowing the resistance to control me, outsmart me, and win for years. When I turned Pro (and for me, that was when I committed to writing a book a month and actually did it), then I found my voice, my self-respect, and my power.

Steven Pressfield is saying that you have to be crazy to be a writer, but if it's in your heart and soul to be one, you must do it with the understanding it demands enormous sacrifice.

It turns out the COVID-19 crisis was a blessing in disguise for my writing because I was no longer suffering from FOMO (Fear of Missing Out) since everyone else was also under quarantine. If it had been a "normal" year, I think I would have struggled more, being forced to turn down invitations and feeling sorry for myself about all the fun things I was missing out on. Because of the lockdown, there wasn't anywhere to go except the grocery store once a week or to see my 84-year-old father and my children.

If you really want to write a book, wake up, STAY IN YOUR PAJAMAS, and start writing.

You may remember the instructions on one of the Monopoly game cards:

Do not pass GO. Do not collect $200.

The player must immediately go to the jail space on the game board, and that player cannot take any other action before going to jail.

If you want to get your book done, take NO other actions.

Just write, even when you think you have nothing to say. I promise, when you sit down and stare at the blank page and push through the *resistance*, you will find words, and new worlds will open up to you.

Don't let your mind trick you. Sit down and write, no matter what. In your pajamas, as soon as you wake up. Take no other actions.

CHAPTER 2
THE PYRAMID

About six months into writing a book a month, I started getting emails, texts, and messages from people I knew, as well as people I didn't know, telling me how great my books were and how amazing my writing was.

Looking back on the first book I published in 2011, I can tell you the difference was like night and day. My writing evolved and got better with every book I wrote.

Unfortunately, aspiring writers have an unrealistic expectation that their first book should be great or perfect. They also believe they should make a million dollars from it.

We Writers Can Be Delusional

Nobel writer, Seamus Heaney, said

> *"When one is learning how to write, one should not expect it to be immediately good."*

I know that's a hard pill to swallow, but the reality is the more we do anything, the better we will get. When you were a baby and took your first steps, you were wobbly and fell down a lot. With practice, you got better.

Stephen King, in his only nonfiction book, *On Writing,* says:

"Writers form themselves into the pyramid we see in all areas of human talent and human creativity. At the bottom are the bad ones. Above them is a group which is slightly smaller but still large and welcoming; these are the competent writers. They may be found on the staff at your local newspaper, on the racks at your local bookstore, and at poetry readings on Open Mic Night… The next level is much smaller. These are really good (great) writers. Above them—above almost all of us are the Shakespeares, the Faulkners, the Yeatses, Shaws, and Eudora Weltys. They are geniuses, divine accidents, gifted in a way which is beyond our ability to understand, let alone attain. Shit, most geniuses aren't able to understand themselves, and many of them lead miserable lives, realizing (at least on some level) that they are nothing but fortunate freaks, the intellectual version of runway models who just happen to be born with the right cheekbones and with breasts which fit the image of an age."

Below is a visual representation of the ***Pyramid of Writers.***

Stephen King says you cannot turn a bad writer into a competent writer. He also says that while it is hard to turn a competent writer into a great writer, it can be done by, "filling your toolbox with the right instruments and through hard work, dedication, and timely help."

In other words, if you're a terrible writer, you can't fix that, but if you're a competent writer, then you can become a great writer.

So how does one do that?

First, sit down and write. Second, be prepared to work hard.

Again, I have to quote Stephen King because this is brilliant:

"…if you don't want to work your ass off, you have no business trying to write well — settle back into competency and be grateful you have even that much to fall back on. There is a muse, but he's not going to come fluttering down into your writing room and scatter creative fairy-dust all over your typewriter or computer station. He lives in the ground. He's a basement guy. You have to descend to his level, and once you get down there you have to furnish an apartment for him to live in. You have to do all the grunt labor, in other words, while the muse sits and smokes cigars and admires his bowling trophies and pretends to ignore you. Do you think this is fair? I think it's fair. He may not be much to look at, that muse-guy, and he may not be much of a conversationalist (what I get out of mine is mostly surly grunts, unless he's

on duty), but he's got the inspiration. It's right that you
should do all the work and burn all the midnight oil,
because the guy with the cigar and the little wings has got
a bag of magic. There's stuff in there that will change
your life. Believe me. I know."

You've probably heard the term *Muse* before. A muse is a person who is the source of inspiration for an artist. Traditionally, they are women – but Stephen King's Muse is a male. It doesn't matter what gender your Muse is. What matters is that if you want the Muse (the inspiration) to show up and you want to go from being a competent writer to being a great writer, you better get ready to work your arse off.

Elizabeth Gilbert, author of *Eat Pray Love,* says,

"Creative living is a path for the brave."

Writing isn't easy because you are essentially in a fight every single time you sit down to do it. Your fears can consume you.

Do any of these fears sound familiar?

- I have no talent
- I'm a bad writer
- I'll be rejected or criticized
- I'll be ridiculed or misunderstood
- No one will read my book(s)
- Others are better than me
- My dreams won't come true

- I don't have the time to write
- I don't have the discipline
- I'll be a "one hit wonder"
- I'll never be a great writer
- My best years have passed me by
- I can't outsmart resistance
- I will be a starving artist

Guess what?

Fear is boring.

Think about that. Fear has nothing interesting to say except:

Stop, Stop, Stop.

By your mere existence, you are original and have something interesting to say. Don't let these fears stop you.

In her book, *Big Magic*, Elizabeth Gilbert wrote the following letter to her fears:

> *"Dearest Fear: Creativity and I are about to go on a road trip together. I understand you'll be joining us, because you always do. I acknowledge that you believe you have an important job to do in my life, and that you take your job seriously. Apparently your job is to induce complete panic whenever I'm about to do anything interesting — and, may I say, you are superb at your job. But I will also be doing my job on this road trip, which is to work hard*

and stay focused. And Creativity will be doing its job, which is to remain stimulating and inspiring. There's plenty of room in this vehicle for all of us, so make yourself at home, but understand this: Creativity and I are the only ones who will be making any decisions along the way. I recognize and respect that you are part of this family, and so I will never exclude you from our activities, but still—your suggestions will never be followed. You're allowed to have a seat, and you're allowed to have a voice, but you are NOT allowed to have a vote. You're not allowed to touch the road maps; you're not allowed to suggest detours; you're not allowed to fiddle or touch the radio. But above all else, my dear old familiar friend, you are absolutely forbidden to drive."

If you want to write books, do NOT give in to your fears. Do not provide them with maps or allow them to take you on detours away from your writing path, and most importantly, never let them drive.

Your mission is to write in spite of your fears, work your arse off, and become a great writer. You no longer have time to think small.

CHAPTER 3
COMBINATORY PLAY

Albert Einstein would often take a break and play the violin when solving a difficult mathematical problem or puzzle. He could usually find the answer he was looking for after a few hours of sonatas.

Once when Elizabeth Gilbert was struggling with a book she was writing, she signed up for a drawing class to open up another *creative channel* within her mind. She couldn't draw very well, but that didn't matter. The important thing was to stay in communication with *artistry* at some level.

Einstein called this "combinatory play," which is the act of opening up one mental channel by dabbling in another.

When I get stuck with my writing, I like to bake cookies, cakes, pies, or other culinary creations.

Michele Cassou and Stewart Cubley, authors of *Life, Paint and Passion*, say this about play:

> *"Play is one of the most basic and primitive elements of the human psyche, and ultimately art is simply a deep and essential play."*

If you look at writing as *play* and an act of *discovery*, you won't take it so seriously, which is what the *resistance* wants you to do.

As children, we had the instinct to play, but as adults, we've traded that in for a life of stress, high productivity, and the feeling that we are not enough and will never be enough no matter how much we do.

When you allow yourself the space to *play*, something deep inside you relaxes, and you suddenly wake up and remember you have the right and instinct to create without guilt or shame.

We were born to create and play.

Elizabeth Gilbert says,

> *"Not expressing creativity turns people crazy."*

The Gospel of Thomas says,

> *"If you bring forth what is within you, what you bring forth will save you. If you don't bring forth what is within you, what you don't bring forth will destroy you."*

If you are actively creating something, then you are probably NOT *actively destroying* something in your life. Funny how that works.

People often say, "I have nothing to say," or "I don't know what to write about."

Great! That's the perfect place to start. With nothing.

When you have nothing to start with, you start with yourself – your intuition and imagination – and you give yourself permission to explore.

The idea for this book came to me when my logical mind was turned off in the middle of the night. All of a sudden, the title came to me, and I jumped out of bed to write it down. Then, I went back to bed. A few minutes later, the subtitle came to me, so I got up again and wrote it down. Then, the 12 chapter titles came to me, so, once again, I got up to write those down.

The creative mind comes out to play when the logical-egoic mind is asleep. For me, this happens when I am playing, taking a walk, sleeping, or in the shower – any activity that doesn't require me to force ideas.

All of this takes time. Sometimes, I get nervous when it's the 10th of the month, and I haven't made any progress writing my book for that month. I like to start with an outline for my book idea, but if I'm not feeling the energy around that book idea and the words aren't flowing, I take a break and see what else comes up.

That's what happened with this book. I had ten other ideas swirling around in my head that I considered writing for this month's book, such as:

1. How to Find Your Super Powers

2. Finding New Windows When Door Slam Shut

3. Recalibration: How to Find Peace in the Midst of Chaos

4. Playchecks Not Paychecks

5. Turn Your Obsession Into Your Profession

6. The Lazy Woman's Guide to a 6-Figure Income

7. Passion Checks: How to Turn Your Passions Into Cash

8. Secrets of Six Figure Authors

9. Six Things Six-Figure Women Don't Do

10. Massive-Passive Income (*I'm writing this book in 2021*)

I don't have a problem coming up with ideas; I have a problem selecting one idea, and that's where I tend to get stuck. However, because I have a strict deadline to get my book written by the end of the month, I don't have the luxury of staying stuck. I have to pick one idea and move on. What gives me peace of mind though is knowing I can still use the other ideas in the future. I feel better knowing that I'm not permanently eliminating a good idea.

When I can't decide which book to write, I turn to play.

PLAY TIME

Last night, I was babysitting my three-year-old granddaughter. We were singing, dancing, putting on magic shows, playing dress-up, laughing, and having fun. This gave me the space to get out of my head, and when I went to bed, the idea for this book suddenly "came to me."

I may eventually write all of those books listed above when the time is right, but my energy was high for this book, and the words began to flow out of me without me *forcing* them. So I chose this idea for my 12th book!

IDEAS DISAPPEAR IF YOU DON'T ACT ON THEM

If an idea comes to you and you are not ready or available for it, it may leave you to search for a different collaborator.

In her book *Big Magic,* Elizabeth Gilbert tells a funny story of when she had an idea to write a novel about Brazil in the 1960s. The idea was epic and thrilling to her, but it was also daunting. She started preparing to write the book, clearing her calendar, declining social invitations, ordering books about Brazil, studying Portuguese, keeping track of notes, and the outline started to take shape.

A few months later, a real-life drama derailed her from writing this book. She put the book away and decided she would have to get back to it later.

When she was ready to get back to the novel two years later, she discovered her energy around writing that novel was completely gone. She explains it this way,

> *"The idea had grown tired of waiting, and it had left me.*
> *If inspiration is allowed to unexpectedly enter you, it is*
> *also allowed to unexpectedly exit you."*

An example of this is when Elizabeth Gilbert met writer Ann Patchett, and they became instant friends, but never discussed the novel that she started to write. Not once. Ironically, Ann later wrote a novel with an almost identical story line.

Elizabeth says,

> *"...ideas do have a conscious will, that ideas do move from soul to soul, that ideas will always try to seek the swiftest and most efficient conduit to the earth (just as lightning does)."*

If you lack ideas or are stuck choosing between several, I recommend getting back to the childhood art of play. Take your left brain out of the equation and watch the ideas flow in.

Go play now.

Remember, when ideas flow in, they can easily flow out if you don't act on them.

I started keeping a "title notebook" several years ago because titles come to me all the time. I regularly read them, and many have lost their energy, and therefore, I lack the vigor needed to write them.

I believe in writing about topics that give you energy.

Even if you have energy about a topic, writing is still scary because much of it is unknown. If you want to write, get used to not knowing where you are going, because that's where the magic is.

Writing is an act of discovery.

As the famous writer Joan Didion once said,

> *"I don't know what I think until I write about it."*

Play. Write. Discover.

CHAPTER 4
THE CUE

A few years ago, I purchased an elliptical machine to get in better shape. I had a 5,000 square-foot house with many rooms I could have put the elliptical in (the spare bedroom, finished basement, or the sunroom). I decided to put it in my bedroom, at the end of my bed, so it would be the first thing I saw when I opened my eyes in the morning.

That was the best decision I ever made because it worked. You know the saying, "Out of sight, out of mind." If I had put the elliptical in another room, I know I would have forgotten about it and rarely used it.

SYSTEMS CREATE HABITS

From reading James Clear's amazing book, *Atomic Habits*, I learned that the cue is an important part of the habit-building system.

Below is an overview of how to build a habit according to James Clear:

"The process of building a habit can be divided into four simple steps: cue, craving, response and reward. This four-step pattern is the backbone of every habit, and your brain runs through these steps in the same order each time.

First, there is the cue. The cue triggers your brain to initiate a behavior. It is a bit of information that predicts a reward. Our prehistoric ancestors were paying attention to cues that signaled the location of primary rewards like food, water, and sex. Today, we spend most of our time learning cues that predict secondary rewards like money and fame, power and status, praise and approval, love and friendship, or a sense of personal satisfaction.

Cravings are the second step, and they are the motivational force behind every habit. Without some level of motivation or desire—without craving a change—we have no reason to act. What you crave is not the habit itself, but the change in state it delivers.

The third step is the response. The response is the actual habit you perform, which can take the form of a thought or an action. Whether a response occurs depends on how motivated you are and how much friction is associated with the behavior…

Finally, the response delivers a reward. Rewards are the end goal of every habit. The cue is about noticing the reward. The craving is about wanting the reward. The response is obtaining the reward. We chase rewards because they serve two purposes: (1) they satisfy us and (2) they teach us."

I didn't know about the four steps to creating a habit when I put the elliptical in my bedroom. It just made sense to me that if it was in a room I didn't spend much time in, I would quickly forget about it.

If you DON'T want to write a book, then ignore cues, and you'll quickly forget that you ever wanted to write a book.

However, if you want to get your book done and out to the world, the most critical step in this habit creation system is the cue.

My *cue* involves setting up my writing station on my dining room table with my laptop, the books I'll be quoting from, a notebook, and a pen. I see my writing station when I get a cup of tea in the morning.

I've discovered that when I clean up my writing station, I quickly forget to write. When I have the cue, I always sit down and start writing first thing in the morning, in my pajamas, before I do anything else.

It is 12 days before Christmas right now, and I'm thinking of all the errands I need to run. However, instead of running those errands, I'm writing two chapters of this book first. As a reward, I will spend the rest of the day shopping and running my Christmas errands.

My motivation is to get my 12th book written and published by the end of the year. I am also motivated by the income I generate from every book I write. My goal is to hit six figures in passive income by this time next year.

My passion for writing books is high because books have transformed my life and saved my life. I wouldn't be here without books, and I know the power of how one book, one page, or one sentence in a book can change a person's life.

WRITING SPACE IDEAS

If you don't live alone as I do (my daughter and granddaughter have moved into their own house now), you may need to find a special place in your home to set up a writing station that everyone will respect and you can see as soon as you wake up in the morning.

We all need motivation to write. Making money is a great motivator. Eventually, that money can support you and give you the time freedom you need to write more books and ultimately impact more people.

Here are a few inspirational pictures below to inspire you to create your own writing station:

SETTING UP YOUR WRITING STATION

If you work from home, it's a good idea to have a separate writing station than where you do your *everyday* work.

I use a spare bedroom as my formal office where I do client work, but I don't want to write in that same space. I prefer a more creative place with a view. Right now, I'm looking out my windows in my dining room at the stunning views of the Chesapeake Bay. Nature inspires me. I have lots of natural light and space in this room, and I love it; it makes me happy.

Before I started writing in my current space, I sat at a small writing desk in my bedroom, which also had a view of the water. However, I outgrew that desk because I needed more space to spread out with my notes and other books I was referencing.

FIND A WRITING SPACE THAT INSPIRES YOU

Once you have set up your writing space and start writing consistently, you will have created a writing habit, and it will start to come automatically.

The difference between being an amateur and a pro is that a pro takes the time to create a space to write that honors their creativity.

James Clear says,

> *"Once a habit has been encoded, the urge to act follows whenever the environmental cue appears."*

The cue has a lot of power, so don't underestimate it.

Think about some of the *automatic cues* you have every day. Your toothbrush is a cue for you to brush your teeth. The pile of bills on the table is a cue for you to pay them. The pile of laundry is a cue for you to wash clothes. The book you just bought on the side table is a cue for you to read it.

I have a friend who is obsessive/compulsive and likes everything put away; his house looks like it should be in a fancy magazine. It's picture-perfect. For me, that doesn't work when it comes to my writing. I need to see the cue every day so that I can get my writing done. Of course, if I have visitors, I'll clean off my dining room table and put everything away. But as soon as the company leaves, it all comes back out!

James Clear says we mentally assign habits to the locations in which they occur: the bedroom, bathroom, office, gym, etc. Each location develops a connection to certain habits and routines. Instead of thinking about your environment as filled with objects, start thinking about them as filled with relationships.

James Clear goes on to say,

> *"Want to think more creatively? Move to a bigger room, a rooftop patio, or a building with expansive architecture. Take a break from the space where you do your daily work, which is also linked to your current thought patterns… When you can't manage to get to an entirely new environment, re-define or re-arrange your current one."*

I think more creatively when I can look out at the water, see nature and when I am in a space with a lot of natural light. I also love to play relaxing music in the background when I'm writing.

Without an inspired writing space and a cue for you to see every day, you won't complete your writing. Set up your cue now and watch your writing habit flourish.

CHAPTER 5
CREATIVE IDLENESS

In her book, *If You Want to Write*, author Brenda Euland says:

> *"If good ideas do not come at once, or for a long time, do*
> *not be troubled at all. Wait for them. Put down the little*
> *ideas however insignificant they are. But do not feel,*
> *anymore, guilty about idleness and solitude."*

In the modern world we live in, it's almost a sin to be idle—to *not* be productive every moment. If you don't want to write books, you should stay busy and not allow yourself the gift of *creative idleness*.

However, if you want to write books, you need to activate your imagination, which happens when YOU allow yourself to be creatively idle.

So, what does creative idleness mean exactly?

Let's first define what it is NOT. It is NOT to be pressed and duty-driven all the time. It is NOT worrying, thinking about the future, and being anxious.

To access our imagination, we need the *dreamy idleness* that children have, like when you:

- Walk alone for a long time

- Lie in bed staring out the window at the stars or the trees blowing in the wind
- Dig in the garden
- Take a long drive in the country by yourself
- Play the piano

Good ideas come slowly. More ideas will come to you when you are tranquil, clear, and unstimulated.

In elementary school, all of my teachers wrote the same thing on my report cards:

"Michelle daydreams too much."

I now see daydreaming as one of my superpowers because it helps me write.

Euland explains,

> *"What we write today slipped into our souls some other*
> *day when we were alone and doing nothing".*

In other words, what you are writing today, you thought and created in your idle time, some other day.

Writers need solitude and long breaks from talking and busyness in order to create. Of course, there is a place for talking and busyness, but if you want to write books, you need to honor your imagination, and that comes from not thinking and not talking.

Inspiration does not come like a lightning bolt but comes very slowly and quietly.

Julie Cameron, author of the bestselling book, *The Artist Ways,* says:

> *"There, caught between the dream of action and the fear of failure, shadow artists are born."*

This happens when the artistic urges of our artist child are ignored or suppressed. Well-intentioned adults tell us to "Stop daydreaming" and force us to take our heads out of the clouds.

Being an artist requires a lot of nurturing to honor and protect our inner artistic child. We can do this by allowing time for daydreaming and creative idleness.

Julia Cameron has two primary tools for creative recovery – the Morning Pages and the Artist Date.

The Morning Pages

The Morning pages are simply writing three pages of stream of consciousness thoughts immediately upon waking up in the morning.

Natalie Goldberg, in her book, *Writing Down the Bones,* says,

> *"First thoughts have tremendous energy. First thoughts are unencumbered by ego, by that mechanism in us that tries to be in control, tries to prove the world is permanent and solid, enduring, and logical."*

There is power in writing first thing in the morning because often we get what Julia Cameron calls "Marching Orders," which are directives from the Universe. I've received many amazing ideas for my books in my morning pages.

The Artist Date

Think of the Morning Pages as sending (notifying the universe of your dreams, dissatisfaction, hopes, etc.). The Artist Date is about receiving (opening yourself to insight, inspiration, and guidance).

Julia's Description of an Artist Date

"An artist date is a block of time, perhaps two hours weekly, especially set aside and committed to nurturing your creative consciousness, your inner artist. In its most primary form, the artist date is an excursion, a play date that you preplan and defend against all interlopers. You do not take anyone on this artist date but you and your inner artist, a.k.a. your creative child. That means no lovers, friends, spouses, children—no taggers-on of any type…

Your artist is a child. Time with a parent matters more than monies spent. A visit to a great junk store, a solo trip to the beach, an old movie seen alone together, a visit to an aquarium or an art gallery—these cost time, not money. Remember, it is the time commitment that is sacred."

For years, I taught the *Artist Way* class at Unity church, and many successful business people would attend because they were all starved for creativity. I know this feeling very well because after working 17 long years in the legal field, I too felt completely drained of creativity.

We nurture our inner artist child by spending time in solitude with them and doing activities such as – taking a long walk, going on a solitary hiking expedition, or enjoying a sunrise or sunset at the beach.

To write and access our imagination, we need more playful inflow!

Julia also talks about Artist Dates as "filling the well," meaning that we feed our brain images instead of words. Art is an image-based system, so when we go on solo artist dates, we feed our artist brain with colors, sounds, smells, and sights.

DISTRACTIONS ARE A WRITER'S ENEMY

Carl Jung was a successful lecturer and psychologist who built a retreat in 1922; it was a two-story basic stone house called *The Tower*. Jung described it this way,

> *"In my retiring room, I am by myself… I keep the key*
> *with me all the time; no one else is allowed in there except*
> *with my permission."*

Jung's daily ritual, according to journalist Mason Currey in his book *Daily Rituals,* was to rise at 7 a.m., eat breakfast, and write in his private office for two undistracted hours. His afternoons included meditations or long walks on the country-side. There was no electricity at *The Tower*, so Jung used oil lamps for light and a fireplace for heat.

It would be easy to see *The Tower* as a vacation home for Jung, but in the context of his career, the lakeside retreat was not an escape from his professional life but a way to advance it.

Carl Jung was one of the most influential thinkers of the twentieth century, and to do his deep work, he had to prioritize his solitude and eliminate distractions.

Distractions are the Biggest Block to Writing

I just looked at my phone, and since I started writing two hours ago, I've received five text messages, three phone calls, over a dozen social media notifications, and fifteen emails. I don't keep my phone with me when I write. I also make sure I turn off all notifications and set it to silent, so I don't hear anything. If my phone was turned on or sitting next to me, I would never get any writing done.

Our addiction to technology and phones is so strong that when we put our phones in another room, we feel as if a part of us is missing, and we may even feel anxious.

In her book, *How to Break Up With Your Phone*, author Catherine Price says,

> *"Breaking up with your phone means giving yourself a chance to stop and think. It means noticing which parts of your relationship are working and which parts are not. It means setting boundaries between your online and offline lives."*

If you want to write books, you must set boundaries, not only people but also with technology.

Neal Stephenson, author of dozens of books, explains it this way:

> "If I organize my life in such a way that I get lots of long consecutive, uninterrupted time-chunks, I can write novels. If I instead get interrupted a lot, what replaces it. Instead of a novel that will be around for a long time, there is a bunch of email messages that I have sent out to individual persons."

It's hard to write books with fragmented attention, yet it's become the norm.

We need long periods of uninterrupted time to write books. I've found that getting up and writing in my pajamas before taking any other actions works well.

One of my clients is a full-time psychologist and has written ten books. He writes from 10 p.m. to 2 a.m. every night and is consistent with his writing.

If you write late at night or early in the morning, you will likely have fewer interruptions and distractions. If you can't do early morning or late evening, you must set strict boundaries and minimize all technology and human distractions.

If you find yourself staring at the blank page with nothing to write about, try adding artist's dates and creative idling to your life. I hereby give you permission to stare into the sky, take long walks to commune with nature, and nurture your inner artist child!

CHAPTER 6
ENERGY VAMPIRES

I know first-hand what an energy vampire is because I dated one for four years; he was what mental health professionals would call a *narcissist*. It was a very toxic relationship, and at the end of those four years, I was emotionally, spiritually, physically, and mentally drained.

When we think of vampires, we might think of someone that comes in the middle of the night while you're sleeping, makes a small incision on your neck, and begins to suck out your blood a little at a time. Your blood gives them life.

Energy vampires do the same thing—they suck out your life force a little at a time, and often we don't even realize it's happening. We just know we feel drained every time we interact with them.

I broke up with this *narcissist* 14 times; he didn't want to let go. Why would he? He was feeding off me to get his narcissistic supply. I won't go into all the details about narcissism here, but it is a serious mental disorder.

If you *don't* want to write a book, then keep all the energy vampires in your life, and I can assure you that you won't have the energy to get your book done.

However, if you are committed to writing your book, you MUST remove all the energy vampires in your life. If it is a family member that you can't remove altogether, you absolutely must minimize contact with them.

Life coach and author Cheryl Richardson says,

> *"A high-quality life has more to do with what you REMOVE from it than what you ADD to it."*

So, how do you know if you have an Energy Vampire in your life?

I'm not a psychologist, counselor, or therapist, but I would say that one feels consistently drained or bad when you interact with that person.

Energy Vampire Red Flags:

- Highly critical of you

- Passive-aggressive

- They don't support your dreams and goals

- They're only interested in themselves

- They talk in circles

- They stir up arguments all the time

- They make you doubt your own perceptions (gaslighting)

- Emotionally unavailable

- Lack the ability to learn and grow

- Are verbally and/or physically abusive

- Love pushing your buttons (which is how they get their supply)

- Make promises but never follow through

- Are takers, not givers (you are the giver in the relationship)

- They don't respect you or your boundaries

I dealt with many of these issues during those difficult four years. If someone in your life is draining you, minimize time with them, or remove them from your life completely if possible. Otherwise, you won't have the creative energy needed to write.

In their book, *Wired to Create,* authors Scott Barry Kaufman and Carolyn Gregoire say:

> *"Solitude is an essential element of self-discovery and emotional maturity, and the reflection undertaken in its company can give rise to our most profound personal and creative insights. Being alone forces us to reflect upon all aspects of ourselves—even those parts that we normally choose to leave un-examined."*

If you have an energy vampire in your life, your thoughts will be ALL about them, even if you have some solitude. When you have a narcissist in your life, you may find yourself *ruminating,* which means that you have excessive repetitive thoughts about these negative experiences, which will ultimately prevent you from writing.

I didn't write any books during these four years when I was interacting with this energy vampire. What helped me get out of this toxic relationship was: going no-contact, working with professionals, and reading many books about narcissists and sociopaths. Once I was healed and out of this relationship, then my creativity re-emerged!

My life and my business began to thrive. I'll be honest, it took about two years to heal from this toxic relationship, but once I did, I started writing a book a month, took on more clients, and my income doubled!

We don't realize how much energy we give to others and wonder why we can't find the time or space to write.

It's time for YOU to clean house. Who do YOU need to minimize contact with or remove completely from your life? Be radically honest. Who is draining your energy and sucking the life out of you?

You have a difficult choice to make if you want to write books. Remember that writing requires great sacrifice. You have to make deductions from your life if you want to add writing books to your life.

We need solitude for our ideas to develop. The presence of others can inhibit this process, especially if they are highly toxic people like energy vampires are.

MORE BENEFITS TO WRITING

Another interesting benefit from writing is that you will find lost parts of yourself, learn about who you are on a deeper level, discover what you believe, and what your truth is.

I think that's why many people fear writing – it's an act of self-discovery.

But you can't get to that act of self-discovery with energy vampires slowly sucking your energy away.

One of my favorite books is *This Time I Dance: Trusting the Journey of Creating the Work You Love* by Tama J. Kieves, a Harvard graduate and left a thriving law practice to follow her dream of being a writer and teacher.

Tama describes leaving her law practice here:

"One day I was a fancy-shmancy corporate attorney with a Harvard law degree cruising down partnership track. The next day, while vacationing on a California beach, the rhythm of the crashing waves inspired a slowed-down moment of self-connection, revealing a stunning summons from within. I found myself promising to leave my powerhouse profession and ramble on more beaches, scramble after wonder, get to know myself again—live before I died—explore all my imaginable reaches. Needless to say, this seamless "plan" didn't seem too lucid or plausible. I didn't have a rich husband to support me—any husband for that matter—no back-up plan, no truly grand faith, and no idea what I would do with an unstructured hour, much less the rest of my life."

Tama's energy vampire was her JOB. It wasn't a person, but an entity; energy vampires come in all shapes and sizes.

After that time-out to the beach in California, Tama left her law practice and became a waitress at the Paradise Café, which gave her the space and solitude she needed to explore her love of writing. She moved to her dream hideaway in the mountains and began writing her first book. She also taught adult education classes in creative writing and offered private seminars and retreats. She went on to lecture, travel, and write more books. She embraced the adventure, but it all began with a huge act of faith – leaving her corporate job that was sucking the life out of her.

It Takes An Intermission to Find Your Mission

You might need an intermission to find your mission, too. I'm not saying you need to travel to the beaches of California, but taking a few days off from your structured life can open up space so you can begin to hear that small, quiet voice inside and re-connect with your dreams.

We are experts at ignoring ourselves and settling for crumbs, but a life of inspiration will come calling sooner or later. You can choose to be practical or magical, but you can't choose both.

Tama describes what happened when she left her law practice,

"By the time I left law, I practically couldn't breathe anymore. I sensed my spacious office shrinking, my file folders sulking, smirking and accusing, and the phones ringing louder. With each passing day. I knew I had to escape that marble-lined, cream-colored elective incarceration."

That is exactly how I felt when I left my 17-year career in the legal field to follow my dreams of writing and teaching. Tama and I have another thing in common: we both wrote our first book ten years after we knew we wanted to be writers.

I'm writing this book to save you from wasting ten years *not* writing. Remove whatever drains you and create the space for your writing and your creative practice now.

You might be saying, "Well, I hate my job, and it drains me, but I have to pay my bills, so what should I do?"

Like Tama, you should get a job that pays the bills but doesn't demand all of your time, energy, and life force. There is a big difference. Tama's legal job required everything, and she was beyond drained. She didn't have a moment to herself. Her life was her work.

As a waitress, she waited tables in the evenings and bought herself daylight hours to walk in the park, write in cafes, and pray to the bliss gods that she could someday find meaning and cash in the same place.

Self-Discovery Became Her New Career

Tama says when we consciously let go of what tires us, what inspires us will take its place. But the key is you have to "let go of what tires you," and those are the energy vampires in your life. Get rid of them!

I, too, was drained after spending 17 years in the legal field. As fate would have it, I was "let go" from the law firm where I worked. My manager said to me, "Michelle, the department you work in is being restructured, and your job no longer exists." That was code for, "You make too much money, you're fired."

It was a blessing in disguise as I was miserable but didn't dare leave because I was unsure what else I could do to support myself and my three young children as a single mom.

Guess what?

I figured it out because my back was against the wall. Within a short time, I became a freelance writer for the local newspaper and taught classes at adult education centers and the community college. Essentially, I started creating multiple streams of income.

Then I found my "freedom job," which was in outside sales. I worked 20-25 hours a week and made six figures. That freedom job gave me the space and solitude I needed to create and start writing, and that's when I started my very first online business, www.becomea6figurewoman.com. Eventually, that evolved into selling online courses, coaching, website design, SEO services, copywriting, ghostwriting, and more, which all led me to launch a new business around my passion for books:

www.bestsellingauthorprogram.com

I came full circle, but it didn't need to take me ten years to write a book, and it shouldn't take you ten years to write a book.

Remove the energy vampires in your life and you will create a life of freedom, creativity, inspiration, and joy.

When you adventurize your life, you will have something to write about.

Don't surrender your power to energy vampires—they are thankless, unappreciative, and want to take you down. Get rid of them, and you will flourish!

CHAPTER 7
CONSUMPTION VS. CREATION

Basho, the great seventeenth-century Haiku master, once said,

"If you want to know about a tree, go to the tree."

If you want to be a great writer, read great books. If you don't want to write books, don't read books.

Stephen King says the Great Commandment for writers is,

"Read a lot. Write a lot."

If I wanted to write a memoir, I would start reading memoirs.

Many successful musicians talk about their influences: great songs, great music, and other great musicians.

Great writing influences us and helps us evolve; the more we read quality writing, the better we become at the art of writing.

Over the years, I've talked to people who wanted to write a book in a specific genre, but when I asked what their favorite books in that genre were, they didn't have an answer because they never read any.

I was talking with a potential client who wanted to write a novel. When I asked him what his favorite novels were in this genre, he didn't have any because, as it turns out, he wasn't a reader.

Then, a month later, he sent me a novel he quickly wrote and I sent it over to my editor to review. According to her, it was not "publishable" without a lot of work. It needed a complete over-haul or re-write. Sadly, the author didn't want to invest the time, energy, or money to work with an editor in order to create a publishable manuscript. He put the project on the back burner and eventually forgot about it.

Invest Time, Energy, and Money If You Want to be Successful

I write non-fiction books because those are the types of books I read. I would say I read 50-100 non-fiction books each year.

I'm sure some people can sit down and write without ever having taken a writing course or reading other books in their chosen genre—but for the majority of us, that's not the case.

You're not reading other people's books to copy them, but for inspiration. By recognizing great writing, you will be able to produce great writing.

I have a client right now who is writing a parenting book, and I can assure you there is nothing on the market like it; she wrote something very unique. She was influenced by reading *great* parenting books and also by reading *bad* parenting books. After seeing so much bad advice on the market, she felt obligated to help parents with her knowledge.

So, reading bad books can influence you to create something better.

CONSUMPTION VS. CREATION

Now that we covered reading well-written books, it's time to talk about reading deprivation.

When I taught *The Artists Way* classes, reading deprivation was week four of the 12-week process of recovering your creativity. I hated reading deprivation week because reading was my life, but I soon discovered reading could also prevent you from being a creator.

Julia Cameron explains it this way:

> *"Reading deprivation is a very powerful tool—and a very frightening one. Even thinking about it can bring up enormous rage. For most blocked creatives, reading is an addiction. We gobble up the words of others rather than digest our own thoughts and feelings, rather than cook up something of our own."*

It was hard for me to give up reading because I was literally addicted to reading, and without a doubt, I wasn't "cooking up something of my own."

So if you're an avid reader, I applaud you. However, if you want to write books, you have to balance consumption with creation. You may need to pause reading in order to start creating.

Speaker and bestselling Author Matthew Hurtado explains reading addiction as an *addiction to negativity* in his YouTube video which I am paraphrasing here.

There's this little disconnect…most people when they watch trainings… and they learn from books, etc., what they do is they mentally process, as if they are doing it. They take in the information and they get a sense of accomplishment, because they took the information in, but there really wasn't any execution or any application of it, so they're not actually doing it… So the disconnect is that when people get in this virtual reality study mode, they take in all this data, and they just get so addicted to it…like'… what's new, what's fresh, it's a new day, I gotta get some new content.'

What they really want to do is to feel the tension, the tension of the polarities of life, the good and evil, the struggle, the drama; they want to be caught in that drama because that's where they feel alive. It's a sense of purpose, it's adrenaline, it's an addiction to negativity really. That's the human condition overall… Within that realm, there is this massive spread, this chasm between where a person says they want to be and where they actually are. They occupy the activity of getting there, by taking in other people's content… it's almost like they are living vicariously through the books and the audios, and the people they listen to.

And so It brings a sense of temporary comfort. And now this sense of temporary comfort is no different than having a cocktail every night. It gives you a little bit of an escape from the real world, and you get this temporary escape from the world, but it brings about a long-term consequence which is the price of self-esteem that is lost. This is the little thing under the radar that doesn't get checked until it's too late…this is what happens when people want to pursue their dreams and their goals; is that it becomes an information-gathering phenomenon. And they believe that since they have the information in their computer brain, that they've actually done it. But there is a massive difference between actually doing it and thinking you know how to do it. See, you don't know how to do anything unless you've executed it."

Hearing Matthew say this reminded me of why I hated reading deprivation week. Reading gave me an adrenaline high – taking in all this new information made me feel alive. I did execute some of what I was reading and learning, but mostly I lived vicariously through books and authors.

I bring this up because I know some people don't read anything, some read a moderate number of books, and some, like me, have a reading addiction that is or can become a block to their creativity.

When I started writing a book a month, I conscientiously cut down on how much I was reading. I know now that the more I read, the less I write. Instead of one or two books a week, I now only read one or two books a month.

Where do you fall on the reading (consumption) vs. writing (creating) spectrum?

If you want to write consistently, you have to find a balance. Everyone is different, so you could eliminate reading while you are writing, minimize how much you read, or limit yourself to reading books only in the genre in which you are writing.

I attended Barbara Winters's *Making a Living Without a Job*, class years ago. She also wrote a book about that, and says:

> *"If you want to be an expert on something,*
> *read ten books about it."*

Like Matthew Hurtado explains, "If you're just reading to consume other people's material and you don't execute on it, you probably have an addiction."

I'm all for reading and doing research to write books, but our minds are tricksters, and the resistance shows up in many clever ways that block us from our creative work.

In the past year, I've started writing half a dozen books that I didn't complete because more research on the topic was needed. However, I didn't have the luxury of time since I was writing a book a month.

When we give ourselves the luxury of time, we may find ourselves endlessly reading, researching, and studying the topic without ever completing the manuscript.

I seriously recommend every writer spend at least one year writing a book a month – you will learn so many valuable lessons. After a year, you can decide how you want to proceed. Maybe you will continue writing a book a month, or perhaps you'll write a book each quarter or year.

I like writing a book a month because it forces me to write what I know and select topics that don't require vast amounts of research. Remember how Elizabeth Gilbert spent two years researching topics for her novel, only to lose energy and passion when it came time to sit down and write the book.

Writing faster is better for many reasons. It may not be possible for every type of book, but it definitely helps writers who are blocked and unable to write.

There are other books I would like to write that will take more than a month to complete, but right now, the book a month system works for me. It's teaching me to be disciplined, not procrastinate, and to execute. It's also created $3,000 a month in passive income, which is a great motivator!

WRITERS CAN FOOL THEMSELVES

Many coaches talk about clients who go through their videos and online training but never execute on the content.

After leaving the legal field, I spent years attending writer's conferences, reading books about writing, and hanging out with other writers, but I wasn't writing. I didn't write a book for over ten years.

I don't know why I didn't write at the time.

In her book, *Writing For Your Life*, Deena Metzger says:

"To undertake to write is to set out on a journey into the self."

I think we have WRITERS BLOCK because we want to avoid the journey into the self at all costs.

Surrendering to the creative process so you can write books is not an easy process. It takes a lot of courage to create and to be vulnerable.

The more you write, the more you will find your voice. It is probably somewhere between revealing too much and hiding too much – revealing vs. concealing.

Readers are writers but can also be blocked creatives. If you're not writing, take the time to examine and modify your reading habits.

CHAPTER 8
TELEPATHY

Many musicians, writers, painters, sculptors, and other artists talk about being a conduit for their work. You might hear them say things like:

- It came to me out of nowhere

- I saw it in a vision

- The words came to me in the middle of the night

- It was like I was taking dictation

Book titles, chapter titles, complete outlines, and introductions often come to me in the middle of the night. I have learned never to wait until morning to jot these ideas down, and instead, I get up and start writing. If I wait until morning, the information vanishes.

Where do these visions and ideas come from?

Some say they come from God; others say they come from connecting with a muse. But really, it's just putting yourself in a place to receive.

Here are some thoughts from Stephen King's amazing book *On Writing*:

"Writers were blessed stenographers taking divine dictation…"

Julia Cameron, author of *The Artist's Way*, says:

> *"The hand of God is moving through your hand as you write. It is very powerful."*

When you get into the flow, write consistently, show up to the blank page day after day, then you will begin to receive information, and consequently start taking "divine dictation."

In my experience, getting into this receiving mode involves preparation with things like:

- Honoring your creativity

- Showing up to write every day

- Creating a sacred space to write

- Coming softly to the blank page; not trying too hard to think of something, but learning to put something down with no strain or force

- Removing the energy vampires from your life

- Embracing the mystery of the creative process

- Being open to receive

- Making room in your life for creative idleness and play

Elizabeth Gilbert, in her book, *Big Magic* says:

"I feel sometimes like my genius sits in the corner and watches me at my desk, day after day, week after week, month after month, just to be sure I really mean it, just to be sure I'm really giving this creative endeavor my whole-hearted effort. When my genius is convinced that I'm not just messing around here, he may show up and offer assistance. Sometimes that assistance will not arrive until two years into a project. Sometimes that assistance will not last for more than ten minutes.

When that assistance does arrive — that sense of the moving sidewalk beneath my feet, the moving sidewalk beneath my words — I am delighted, and I go along for the ride. In such instances, I write like I am not quite myself. I lose track of time and space and self. While it's happening, I thank the mystery for its help. And when it departs, I let the mystery go, and I keep on working diligently anyhow, hoping that someday my genius will reappear.

I work either way, you see — assisted or unassisted – because that is what you must do in order to live a fully creative life. I work steadily, and I always thank the process."

If you want to write books, make a living with your writing, and be creative, you must take a leap of faith. Show up every day to write, and you will be "assisted" from time to time with divine guidance and inspiration, but like Elizabeth Gilbert says, you do the work even if the muse doesn't show up.

When I started doing my Morning Pages, I didn't know what to write about, so I complained a lot –about my job, my current boyfriend, or whatever drama was going on in my life. Once I got that out of my system, ideas started to show up on the pages, and I believe it was because I was showing up consistently.

In her book, *If You Want to Write*, Brenda Euland says,

> *"That is as it should be—though you must sit before your typewriter just the same and know, in this dreamy time, that you are going to write, to tell something on paper, sooner or later. And you also must know that you are going to sit here tomorrow for a while, and the next day and on and on, forever and ever."*

Forever and ever sounds like a long time. That's the difference between dabbling in writing and being 100% committed to it. When you honor your commitment to write and show up, it will happen. You can't force it; you just have to let the ideas trickle in.

The hardest part of writing is not knowing what will show up on the page, which can leave you feeling vulnerable. However, if you over-plan and try to "force" and "prepare" everything in advance, your writing may become sterile, dry, and boring.

I like to start my books with a working title and outline, but once I start writing, some of those elements change as new ideas come forth. That's the beauty of the writing process; it's not set in stone.

Writers are Great at Creating Distractions to Avoid Writing

In her book, *Writing Down the Bones*, Natalie Goldberg says:

"Instead people often begin writing from a poverty mentality. They are empty and then run to teachers and classes to learn about writing. We learn writing by doing it. That simple."

Remember what Matthew Hurtado said about living vicariously through others and consuming their materials through classes, books, etc. There is a time and place for studying and learning but know that writers can take it too far and avoid writing for years.

In my Bestselling Author program, I have clients who worked on their book or idea for years (sometimes as much as ten years) and couldn't get it done. Then, after working with me for 8-12 weeks, they have a published #1 bestselling book.

How did that happen?

Because they had accountability and a mid-wife (me) to help them give birth to their book.

In the past, I've hired high-ticket coaches, not because I didn't know what to do, but because I knew I needed an accountability partner to execute on the strategies and ideas in my head.

In fact, I stayed with one coach for four years, knowing I would get distracted from my goals if I was left to my own devices. I needed that accountability, so I kept paying him and I did get the results I wanted.

DO YOU HAVE ACCOUNTABILITY?

Don't join a writer's group and think that is accountability. If you feel that you need an accountability partner, hire a coach, pay good money, and believe me, you'll show up and do the work.

It's interesting to me that when people pay for something, they tend to show up a lot more. I think it's human nature that if we spend a lot of money on something, we see more value in it, and we want a return on our investment.

There are many amazing writer's coaches out there, or you can apply to work with me if you want to get your book done in 12 weeks and become a #1 bestselling author. I only take on two - four clients per month, so space is limited. I know this process works because dozens of my clients, who were stuck with either too many ideas or not enough ideas, all finished their books while working with me.

When I started writing a book a month, I created a 30-day roadmap to help me focus and stay organized. I also wanted to create a new income stream with my books.

Many authors are motivated by the income writing a book a month can potentially create, which is great because that motivation will enable you to get your book written and out into the world. It also removes the opportunity to over-plan, become distracted, or procrastinate—you are on a tight timetable, and you must write and publish your book in 30 days.

The 30-Day Roadmap to Writing a Book a Month:

- **Pre-Pub**: Complete your Annual Publishing Chart before you start writing and consider which books will be in a series, so you can later create box sets.

- **Day 1:** Decide on the book topic and do your keyword research.

- **Day 2:** Create a mind map for your book.

- **Day 3:** Create an outline for your book.

- **Day 4-15:** Write the book (I use block time; do whatever works for you).

- **Days 16-23:** Send the manuscript to the editor (this goes back and forth a few times).

- **Days 24-25:** Finalize your eBook cover and format the final manuscript for the eBook and print.

- **Days 26-27:** Order an ISBN for the print book, write the book description for Amazon and the back cover for the print book.

- **Day 28:** Finalize the print cover (you need the page count, back cover text, and the ISBN to complete this).

- **Days 29-30:** Publish the eBook and print book.

- **Post-Publishing:** Get five reviews, hire promoters, market to your email list, post to social media, and do 1 to 2-day book launch.

- **Post-Publishing:** Set up Amazon Ads (80% of my income comes from my ads).

- **Post-Publishing:** Work on your next book.

Having a timeline may impede creativity for some, but I find my writing is more consistent when following the 30-day road-map so I can write and publish a book every month.

To date, I'm very happy with my results. After writing a book a month for 12 months and launching ten of those 12 books, I have created $3000 in monthly royalties! This never would have happened if I didn't give myself a timeline with strict deadlines to write a book a month.

TIME ISN'T THE PROBLEM

I used to complain that I didn't have "time" to write because I was a single mom with a 9-5 corporate job. Then, after I was let go from the law firm and had all the time in the world to write, I still didn't write!

Time is an excuse we use and a lie we tell ourselves when we don't prioritize our creative life and writing.

After not getting any writing done in six months, I thought, "I need to stop talking to my girlfriends on the phone and write from 9 a.m. until noon every day." And guess what? In six months, I finished writing my very first manuscript, *Woman Take Hold of Your Power*.

In sales there is a saying, "Buyers are liars." I think "Writers are liars," too. We lie to ourselves and create excuses to avoid writing.

Stop telling yourself that you don't have the time, ideas for your book, or anything important or different to say. You have all of that and more. If you want to write books, put yourself on a strict timeline, make it public, and get to work!

CHAPTER 9
THE UNKNOWN KNOWN

I've been advised to, "Write what you know." However, even when you write books on topics you are knowledgeable about, a certain level of the unknown remains. You don't know *exactly* what will come out of you when you sit down to write a book.

We are brought up to fear the unknown, which is why we try to control as many things in our lives as possible. But I can assure you, when writing books, the magic happens in the unknown.

In their book, *Life, Paint and Passion: Reclaiming the Magic of Spontaneous Expression*, authors Michele Cassou and Stewart Cubley talk about the void when teaching their painting classes and workshops:

"People often start their paintings by filling in the background — the whole surface is covered in a few minutes. They may do this out of habit, fear, learned technique, or convenience. Whatever the reason, not a trace of virgin paper is left. I always witness with apprehension, this killing of the void."

The authors go on to say,

"Let yourself rest in the void for a while. Perhaps an impulse will come — say, a little blue area right of center — and you will start with it. Put the brush in that spot and move slowly. Be sensitive to where the brush wants to move. Follow its lead. It

*may feel good to continue carefully, to stay in a limited area.
Live with the uncertainty of what will appear in the
surrounding white space.*

*Don't jump too quickly! This defeats the purpose of the painting
process, which is to put you in a position where you don't know
what to do. Let your feelings be free as you continue to paint the
in the moment, not knowing how to resolve the painting as a
whole. It is living with this uncertainty that begins to open the
intuitive senses. Hidden levels reveal themselves when you rest
quietly in the unknown."*

Surrender to the Unknown and You Will Reach Those Hidden Levels

Many writers advocate starting a book with an outline, which I also recommend, but it is not required.

I've written with and without an outline, and I can finish a book a month when working with an outline. It gives me a little sense of the "known," but there is still a lot *unknown* because I don't know exactly what I'm going to write in each of the chapters, and sometimes the chapters change as I begin to write.

The *void* is the source of all creation, and it applies to your writing as well. Don't try to plan too much because you take away the hidden levels that reveal themselves when you "rest quietly in the unknown."

The unknown is a big part of writer's block. We sit and stare at the blank page and wonder what we should write.

You risk exposure, no matter what you decide to write. You're exposing who you are, what you believe, and what you feel. It can feel dangerous to reveal ourselves in such a personal way to the world, knowing that not everyone will embrace our truth.

We fear the blank page because we are committing to those words once we write them down. Of course, you can change the words, but it still feels scary to write them.

MIND DUMP

I like to use a working outline because our minds are messy, and we have so many thoughts and ideas swirling around for our books. We can go in a million different directions—literally.

I do a mind dump for my chosen topic. For example, my mind dump for this book included the following chapter ideas:

- Embrace being a bad writer
- Walk a lot
- Create solitude
- Remove energy vampires
- Write in your pajamas
- Don't ask permission
- Set deadlines, which are great motivators
- Establish accountability to create action
- Write what you know
- Know your why

- Write out of order

- Start with a great quote or story

- Write your truth

- Know that you will offend others

- Do a mind dump

- Clear your mind

- High consumption equals low creation

When doing a mind dump, you can write each item on Post-It notes and then group them together to create an outline for your book. Not everything you write has to be used in the book, but it gives you a starting point.

You also need to consider who your target reader is if you want to make money with your book.

In his book, *How to Write a Saleable Book: In 10-minute Bursts of Madness*, Nicholas Boothman says:

> *"Writing a book and selling a book are completely separate undertakings. If you get the selling part right, before the writing part happens, your chances of success go through the roof. The biggest little secret of a saleable book is to know who your primary audience is."*

I used to write books without thinking too much about my primary audience. I soon learned that was a big mistake.

Consider the reasons a reader would buy your book instead of other books on the market. Determine who your target reader is first and you will increase your chances of making money with your book exponentially.

Ask yourself, "What exactly does my reader want, and how will they know when they have it?"

Nonfiction readers often want to be entertained and find tools they can use immediately to solve a problem. A saleable book should offer a promise and then deliver on that promise.

DO YOU WANT TO MAKE MONEY?

Let's talk about making money with your book.

Some authors say they don't care about making money; they just want to get the information or message out to the world.

That's great if you're a multi-millionaire, but it costs money to get your message out to the world. It costs money to market your book so readers can find it. Don't fool yourself by thinking you don't need to make money with your book.

Many authors who say they don't expect to make money with their book might be telling themselves that just to avoid being disappointed if their book doesn't make any.

I can tell you as a self-published author that you likely won't make a ton of money from your book on day one; it takes time. Eventually, however, if you get your book on multiple bestsellers list so people can find it, as well as run Amazon ads, then your income from that book will grow.

I've found that nothing happens until I do a proper book launch and get my book out there in a big way. I've included the details for doing book launches in several of my books, including *Self-Publishing Secret Sauce*.

Book Launch Summary

- Pick 1-2 days for your book launch.

- Decide on a free launch or discounted launch of $.99 (kindle only).

- Hire 5-10 book promoters (example: Book Bub, Robin Reads, etc.) to promote your book.

- Ensure your book is in the proper categories so it will rank high on the bestsellers lists during the launch.

- Send an email to your list notifying them of the book launch.

- Schedule hourly social media posts during the launch.

- When the book hits #1 on launch day, take screenshots and create a marketing collage.

- Set up Amazon ads and media interviews.

- Rinse and repeat.

I invest about $1,000 in editing, formatting, cover design, and book launch expenses for every book I write and publish.

Usually, in the first month, I make $50-100 from a book, but sales always snowball after that.

What's amazing about writing a book a month and creating $3,000 in passive income in 12 months is I have exceeded my expected social security income! I talk about this in more detail in my book, *Digital Retirement*.

It's important to understand that not all of your books will do well. Right now, about 75% of my income comes from three of my books (based on current sales for the last 30 days):

- *How to Find Your Passion* – **40.4% of sales**

- *28 Books to $100K* – **18.3% of sales**

- *Digital Retirement* – **16.3% of sales**

- *Stop Living Paycheck to Paycheck* – 7.1% of sales

- *Work From Home and Make 6-Figures* – 4.9% of sales

- All other books – 13% of sales

Even with all the preparation I do to find highly-searched topics based on data from keyword research, coming up with a unique hook, and knowing my target reader, I still don't know which books will take off and which ones will flop.

Elizabeth Gilbert talks about this in her book, *Big Magic,*

"I once wrote a book that accidentally became a giant bestseller, and for a few years there, it was like I was living in a hall of fun house mirrors. It was never my intention to write a giant bestseller, believe me. I wouldn't know how to write a giant bestseller if I tried. (Case in point: I've published six books—all written with equal passion and effort—and five of them were decidedly not giant bestsellers)."

This is why it's a great idea to write more than one book. The data from Written Word Media says that authors with at least 28 books make six figures. You can't put all your eggs in one basket by writing only one book. Many fiction authors write in series, because they know they will gain a following and repeat readers.

If you are stuck NOT getting your book done, do the opposite of what you've been doing. If you haven't been creating an outline, then start with one, and vice versa.

As I said at the beginning of this book, writers are troubled people. We have to trick ourselves into sitting down and writing. I know because I was a stuck writer for ten years, and now, in the last 12 months, I've written 12 books.

I want the same for you. You don't have to write a book a month like me, but it's a good idea if you are stuck. It forces you to fight through the inertia and the "I don't know what to write" excuse. You will get it done because you're on a timeline.

I like having public accountability as well. When I told my clients, family, and friends that I was writing a book a month, two things happened:

1. It became real for me

2. I knew I had to keep my word or I would look like a liar

So, tell the world you're writing a book a month to motivate yourself to get it done and out into the world.

Without a deadline, it may take years to write your book, and by the time you do, it might be out of date. The world is changing rapidly, so when you have an idea for a book, you should write it quickly.

PARKINSON'S LAW

Work expands to fill the time available for its completion. You may have heard of a proverb known as *Parkinson's Law*.

Human beings are complicated. If you give someone a week to complete a 2-hour task, it will increase in complexity and become more daunting to fill the time allotted.

If I said I will give you $100,000 to write a 100-page quality book in seven days, I promise, you would get that book done.

If you don't have a timeline, deadline, or some accountability, you'll fall into the trap of too much time and probably never get your book done.

Yes, the unknown is scary, but when you have a tight timeline, you'll surrender to it and get your book written. Quit believing you must write a perfect book and settle for "good enough," or as bestselling author Seth Godin says, "Always be shipping."

CHAPTER 10
KNOWING YOUR WHY

American painter Robert Henri once said:

"When the artist is alive in any person, whatever his kind of work may be, he becomes inventive, searching, daring, self-expressive creature. He becomes interesting to other people. He disturbs, upsets, enlightens, and opens ways for better understanding. Where those who are not artists try to close the book, he opens it and shows there are still more pages possible."

I believe we are born to create and be constructive. If we're not being *constructive*, we may find ourselves being *destructive*.

While attending a workshop on public speaking years ago, another attendee, a counselor who worked with depressed individuals, said to me, "If you're not expressing yourself, you are probably depressed."

Aside from professional or financial reasons, we have an innate and natural desire to create.

I have a friend who paints and does crafts, not for the purpose of making money, but because it feeds her soul. That is creative living.

We can write just to write because we have a deep desire to express ourselves this way and it feeds our soul.

Elizabeth Gilbert says,

> *"I never wanted to burden my writing with the responsibility of paying for my life. I knew better than to ask this of my writing, because over the years, I have watched so many other people murder their creativity by demanding that their art pay the bills."*

Wow! Murdering your creativity sounds serious. There is a lot of pressure to "perform" if you rely on your book to make money to support yourself.

That's why I love the idea of writing a book a month, which alleviates the pressure. If you put 12 books out into the world in one year, you will create income. At the end of the year, you can then decide whether to continue writing a book a month based on your results (every book and every author's results will be different).

You might be surprised, like I was, to discover your writing income can support you and also allow you to retire early!

Treat it like an experiment, and don't put unnecessary pressure on yourself.

Because my bestselling author program provides me with a 6-figure income, I don't need to pay my bills with my writing income. Like I mentioned earlier, it started out as an experiment to see how much money I could create by writing a book a month. Now that I'm 12 books in, I can tell you creating $3,000 a month in 12 months is super exciting and motivating!

Going into the new year, I plan to create box sets from my 12 books, record some audio books, have a few books translated into other languages and continue writing new books. I want to create a 6-figure income from my writing so I can retire in the next year.

I love the creative process, because it feeds my soul…and now it feeds my bank account – win–win!

So, let me ask you the million dollar question—why do you want to write a book?

Here are some common and valid reasons for writing:

- To tell your story
- To express yourself
- To get an important message out to the world
- Attract new clients to your business
- Become the authority in your niche
- Find a tribe
- Make a living with your writing
- Have fun
- Find out what you believe
- Be of service and help others
- All of the above

There are no right or wrong answers. The point is to simply examine *why* you want to write a book and allow that reason to motivate you to write.

Too many people die with their books inside of them and never get a chance to tell their story. Many of my clients say, "Even if my book helps just one person, it will be worth it."

If you don't get your book written, you won't help anyone.

Books have changed my life and saved my life, which is why I am so passionate about them. Anything that has the power to save someone's life is serious.

Prioritizing your creativity forces you to make the sacrifices necessary to achieve your goals. I could be out doing other things right now, but I'm forgoing those "other things" to write the final chapters of this book and get it done by the deadline.

When I examine my "whys" for writing, I find they have been different at various times in my life. For example, in 2000, when I left the legal field, I felt starved for creative expression and the need to journal and write with no intention of publishing anything. I just needed to get my thoughts, feelings, and emotions on paper, which filled that need to express myself.

Eventually, I did want to write a book and wrote, "*Woman, Take Hold of Your Power: 50 Subconscious Ways Women Give Away Their Power*" to help other women who might be going through something similar.

I have a strong desire to teach what I've learned. Also, I find that I learn more deeply when I teach.

When I began the book a month experiment in January 2020, my *why* was to create a catalog of 28 books (products) and generate a six figure income.

You may have one why or multiple whys, or your whys may change, and that's okay. There is no wrong or right reason to write. You are a human being and, therefore, a creative being.

Brenda Euland, author of *If You Want to Write*, says:

> "*Everybody is talented because everybody who is human has something to express. Try not expressing anything for twenty-four hours and see what happens. You will nearly burst.*"

WARNING: If we don't express ourselves, we can potentially become destructive.

DESTRUCTION KILLS

In her book, *Women Who Run With the Wolves*, author Clarissa Pinkola Estes says,

> "*Or, like Janis Joplin, a woman can try to comply until she can't stand it any longer, and then her creative nature, corroded and sickened by being forced into the shadow, erupts violently to rebel against the tenets of "breeding" in reckless ways that disregard one's gifts and one's very life.*
>
> *...sneaking a life because the real one is not given room enough to thrive is hard on women's vitality. Captured and starved women sneak all kinds of things: they sneak unsanctioned books and music, they sneak friendships, sexual feeling, religious affiliation. They sneak time away from their mates and families. They sneak a treasure into the house. They sneak their writing times, their thinking time, their soul time.*"

If we don't honor our creative selves, that unexpressed energy can become destructive energy and devastate our lives.

Clarissa goes on to say,

> *"You see, there is something in the wild soul that will not let us subsist forever on piecemeal intake."*

If you find yourself "sneaking" a creative life, you're probably in a drought. Find the courage to remove the things draining your energy, so you can repurpose that energy and go forth and create.

We have to create boundaries around our own health and welfare, and our creativity is part of that. Clarissa says,

> *"It's not the joy of life that kills the spirit of the child... it's the lack of it. To hold joy, we may sometimes have to fight for it..."*

Sadly, many women conformed and destroyed their lives – Anne Sexton, Judy Garland, Billie Holiday, and Frida Kahlo. These women were wild and artistic, and their lives ended prematurely and tragically.

Do not conform.

Unhealed wounds can prevent us from creating and setting boundaries around our own health and welfare. A big part of why I didn't write anything for ten years was that I needed to tend to my inner wounds. Once I addressed and healed them, I was able to start creating.

Sometimes, we need to overcome an addiction to self-destruction before we can create. Clarissa explains:

> *"A woman may try to hide from the devastations of her life,*
> *but the bleeding, the loss of life's energy, will continue until*
> *she recognizes the predator for what it is and contains it."*

When we are injured and bleeding, we lose our energy to create.

So what exactly is the predator?

A predator is anything that blocks us from living a creative life of joy. The predator derails us, demolishes our dreams and goals, and decapitates us.

We have a soul-need to express ourselves, but there are many traps out there, such as:

- Not listening to or believing in our intuition
- Putting the opinions, dreams, and desires of others above our own
- Not being able to say NO
- Being a people pleaser and being too nice
- Compliance instead of fighting for our joy and creative life
- Being tamed and put in a cage
- Letting someone else take care of our needs
- False love

- Being naïve

- Poor choices

- Soul famine

- Not having supportive people in our lives

- Having no boundaries

- Too much properness and not enough play

- Conformity

All of these traps have a cost – our dreams, desires, and goals.

We must ask ourselves these hard questions:

- What do I long for?

- What do I crave?

- What do I desire?

- What am I hungry for?

- What do I yearn for?

We must hold out for what we want and what our soul wants. In fact, we must fight for it every day.

CHAPTER 11:
THE PERMISSION MYTH

In her bestselling book, *Nice Girls Still Don't Get the Corner Office*, psychologist Lois P. Frankel says,

"Have you ever noticed that men don't ask permission? They ask forgiveness. My hunch is that women ask permission more out of habit than from really needing someone to give them the green light. It's a variation of playing it safe—but potentially more self-defeating. In our society we expect children, not adults, to ask permission. Every time a woman asks permission to do or say something, she diminishes her stature and relegates herself to the position of a child. She also sets herself up to hear "No."

Are you waiting for someone to give you permission to write your book?

I'm not going to give you permission because you don't need it.

Two decades ago, when I was trying to get a deal with a big NY publishing house, I finally got a call from one of the top five. They were very interested in my manuscript. Here's how the conversation went:

"We love your manuscript, *Woman Take Hold of Your Power,* but this is a self-help book for women, and we need to know what your credentials are.

Credentials?

Yes, do you have a Ph.D. or are you a licensed clinical social worker?

No, I have something better than that.

Really, what is better than a Ph.D.?

Life experience! I wrote that book not from theory, but from my own life and my girlfriends' lives and stories.

Wow, that's really great. Unfortunately, the publishing world is very competitive, and this is a self-help book. Although we really like it, if you had a Ph.D., we would publish it. Since you don't, we will have to pass on it. I hope you understand. It's just business.

I'm sorry to hear that."

End of conversation.

If I could go back 20+ years, I would change one thing about that conversation. I would suggest to the publishing house to enlist someone with a Ph.D. to write the foreword to my book and put his or her name on the cover which would satisfy their requirement for *credentials.*

Even though they didn't publish my book, that conversation was very important to my writing life and career because it gave me validation that my writing was good enough for a big publishing house to call me.

Was I looking for permission to continue writing?

Yes, absolutely. I wanted validation, permission, and someone to tell me my writing was good enough. At the time, I didn't have enough belief in myself. I'm lucky I got it because it led me to where I am today. Without it, I may have stopped writing. I'm not sure.

If you're waiting for validation or permission, you may never get it. Sure, you can send your writing to family and friends, but they will most likely tell you it's great and may not be 100% truthful with you.

An honest editor will tell you the truth. Maybe it needs a little work, a lot of work, or you need to start over.

You wouldn't be reading this book if you didn't want to write books.

There's no Wizard of Oz who is going to grant you permission and give you the green light to become a published author. You have as much right as anyone to write and publish a book.

Think of ten books you have read that have transformed your life.

What if those authors allowed their fears to control them, never got the permission or validation they were seeking, and never published their books?

That would be devastating, wouldn't it?

THE PUBLISHING WORLD HAS CHANGED

Before Amazon's self-publishing platform came along, you had to get through the gatekeepers of the publishing world (literary agents and publishing houses) to get your book published.

It was intimidating, to say the least. I received dozens of rejection letters when I was trying to get a deal for my first book. It is hard to continue when you get a lot of rejections because you start believing your writing isn't good enough after a while.

Now, anyone can self-publish a book on Amazon without needing permission from the gatekeepers.

Many 6-7 figure authors now choose to self-publish and keep 100% of the royalties instead of giving 80% or more to publishers and agents.

*Does being a published author mean
that your writing is good or great?*

Absolutely not.

That's the Catch-22. There are a lot of bad books on Amazon. I always remind my clients that we will put out the best quality book we can, but at the end of the day, the market decides what it likes.

Publishers and literary agents decide which books to publish based on experience, market research, and intuition, but the 80/20 rule applies to them as well. 80% of the books they publish don't do great, and 20% are a financial success. That means 80% of the income and sales come from 20% of their books.

This 80/20 rule is called Pareto's Law, and it's true for many things, including books.

In the last chapter, I showed you that three of my books now account for over 75% of my income. Pretty interesting if you ask me.

It's hard to predict which books will strike a chord with the market; just put your best foot forward and you'll find out soon enough.

Give yourself permission to write books and allow the market to decide if they like it.

BOOK LAUNCHES ARE A MUST

Amazon is a crowded marketplace, and if you don't do a book launch and market your book, it will be invisible on their platform.

I am a big proponent of book launches because readers often go to the bestsellers list when searching for a book to buy. Gone are the days of having BISAC codes only. Amazon has more than 10,000 categories and sub-categories where your book can shine and become a bestseller.

Right now, seven of my books are on the *Women and Business* bestsellers list, and I did that intentionally. I wanted to dominate this category because women are my target audience.

Once you give yourself permission to write books, you should do so very strategically, as I talk about in *28 Books to $100K*. Plan your books for the year and write in 1-3 genres. I encourage my students to plan what books they will write for the entire year, and also to plan to create box sets at the end of the year.

I plan to do this next month since I now have published 12 books this year.

My Box Set Strategy:

BOX SET #1 – AUTHOR BOOKS

- *28 Books To $100k*
- *Digital Retirement*
- *Self-Publishing Secret Sauce*

BOX SET #2 – CAREER/LIFE PURPOSE BOOKS

- *Quit Your Job and Follow Your Dreams*
- *How To Find Your Passion*
- *Work From Home & Make 6-Figures*

BOX SET #3 – INCOME BOOKS

- *Stop Living Paycheck to Paycheck*
- *Make Money While You Sleep*
- *Massive Passive Income (not yet written)*

My good friend and fellow author, Marc Reklau, who has written and published dozens of books and box sets on Amazon, told me his income from his books is $270,000 this year.

That is incredible! Marc is my inspiration!

Imagine if Marc had waited for permission to write and publish his books.

WHY DO SOME OF US BELIEVE WE NEED PERMISSION?

Many of us were taught to respect authority. The gatekeepers of the publishing world were seen as the absolute *authority* for publishing books for so long. We mistakenly still believe we need permission from an *authority*.

I'm here to give you good news – you don't need permission, but you do need courage and bravery to believe in yourself enough to share your thoughts, ideas, and beliefs in a book that will be shared with the world.

I recently watched the *Wizard of Oz* with my three-year-old granddaughter. The main characters each believed that the all-powerful OZ had to give them what they needed. The Scarecrow thought he needed a brain, the tin man thought he needed a heart, and the lion believed he needed courage, but as it turns out, they had everything they needed all along.

Dorothy did too. She thought she needed the red shoes to get home, but "she had the power all along."

You, too, have the power. You don't need permission. No Wizard of OZ or authority needs to bestow these powers upon you. Go forth and write books!

CHAPTER 12
REAL ARTISTS DON'T
HAVE TO STARVE

In his book, *Real Artists Don't Starve*, author Jeff Goins says:

> *"Making a living off your creative talent has never been easier…the ideas of the Starving Artist is a useless myth that holds us back more than it helps us."*

The subtitle of this book is: **12 Things You Should Never Do If You Want to Become an Author and Make a Living With Your Writing**

I intentionally added *Make a Living* because so many people misguidedly believe that you can't or shouldn't try to make a living writing books, and you should only write a book to be of service and help others.

This is very altruistic, but why wouldn't you want to make a living with your writing? How will you pay for the marketing to get your book out to the world? Also, you need to pay your bills so that you have the time-freedom to write. Right?

Starving Artists Don't Inspire Anyone

Money motivates me, and I'm not going to apologize for that. I love teaching, helping others, and being rewarded for sharing my gifts with others, but money buys me freedom and allows me to teach and write more books that help others.

The Health Alliance Plan, an HMO with over half a million members, once asked women what was holding them back from living their perfect life. The #1 answer was *money*.

In her book, *Sacred Success*, author Barbara Stanny defines Sacred Success this way:

> *"Sacred Success is pursuing your Soul's purpose for your own bliss and the benefit of others, while being richly rewarded."*

Accept that it is okay to profit from your gifts and writing books. You don't have to be the most prolific writer in the world to make money. All you need is a 10% edge.

Jill Stanton, founder of www.screwtheninetofive.com, talks about embracing the 10% edge:

> *"The 10% edge is about giving yourself permission to start before you're ready…it's the permission to say I'm 10% further along than these people."*

You don't have to "know it all" to write a book about your knowledge or experience; you only need to be 10% further along than others, giving you the edge.

I wish I had known about the 10% edge when I started my online business, www.becomea6figurewoman.com in 2005. I thought I needed to know it *all* before I could teach.

Slowly, I realized that even when I didn't know it all, I could teach from where I was and there was a group of people who wanted this information because they weren't as far along as I was.

YOUR SPIN MAKES YOUR BOOK UNIQUE

Some people are deterred from writing books because they believe it must be something unique with a topic that has never been written about before.

Not true.

My father always told me that there is nothing new under the sun, but it becomes something new when you put your unique spin on it.

Put Your Spin On It

Share your story, experiences, and knowledge to make your book unique.

My top selling book, *How to Find Your Passion: 23 Questions that Can Change Your Entire Life,* is about finding your passion. When I go to Amazon.com and type "how to find your passion" in the search bar, there are more than 2000 results!

Does that mean I shouldn't write a book about finding your passion because there are already so many books on the market?

Absolutely NOT!

I have something unique to say about this topic. Right now, this is my top-selling book, which generates over 40% of my income! I'm glad I wrote this book and didn't let that misguided belief that I needed to write a book with an original topic.

Of course, it's important to have a unique *hook to your book*, which is something that would influence readers to buy your book instead of other books on the topic. The *hook to your book* allows you to display your creativity and uniqueness.

In my Bestseller Checklist training, I talk about something I call the "Snowflake Hook."

THE SNOWFLAKE HOOK

No two snowflakes are the same. You must create a book that has NOT been done before. How, you ask? Here are some ideas (with actual book titles as examples):

- *Change the Perspective*: "Public Speaking for People Who Hate Public Speaking"

- *Shock Factor*: "The Subtle Art of Not Giving a F*ck"

- *Make up a New Process/Method/System*: "Habit Stacking: 127 Small Changes to Improve Your Health, Wealth & Happiness"

- *Make the Complicated Simple*: "The Index Card: Why Personal Finance Doesn't Have to Be Complicated"

- *Against the Norm*: "The 30-Hour Day: Develop Achiever's Mindset & Habits"

- *Contrary Messaging* – "The Obstacle Is the Way"

- *Solve a Million Dollar Problem*: "Profit First: Transform Your Business from a Cash-Eating Monster to a Money-Making Machine"

- *Mimic the Classics* – "Write and Grow Rich"

A good hook grabs the reader's attention and piques interest! Think outside the box.

So, let's dissect the title of this book, *How NOT to Write a Book.* Which snowflake hooks did I use in my title? Definitely these three:

1. Contrary Messaging

2. Against the Norm

3. Change the Perspective

Most readers would expect the title to be: "How to Write a Book," not "How NOT to Write a Book."

I changed the perspective because so many writers are stuck not writing books. I've been there, so I can share what I learned and how I turned that around.

Remember, you want to find inspiration and be influenced by great books on the market and then create your own version.

Here are some Books and Series that Have a Snowflake Hook:

- Author Amy Morin wrote three books in a series: *13 Things Mentally Strong People Don't Do, 13 Things Mental Strong Women Don't Do,* and *13 Things Mentally Strong Parents Don't Do*

- Timothy Ferris wrote: *The 4-Hour Work Week, The 4-Hour Chef,* and *The 4-Hour Body*

- Robert Kiyosaki wrote a series of Rich Dad books such as: *Rich Dad, Poor Dad, Rich Dad's Guide to Investing, Rich Dad's Cashflow Quadrant, Rich Dad's Increase Your Financial IQ, Rich Dad's Before You Quit Your Job, Rich Dad's Retire Young, Retire Rich, Rich Dad's Guide to Becoming Rich Without Cutting Up Your Credit Cards,* and more!

- Steve Scott writes about Habits in his books: *Habit Stacking, Mindful Relationship Habits, Bad Habits No More,* and *Stack Your Savings to Build the Money Saving Habit.*

- Seth Godin writes dozens of books about sales and marketing: *The Dip, The Purple Cow, Linchpin, All Marketers are ~~Liars~~ Tell Stories, Permission Marketing,* and more.

- Hal Elrod writes dozens of books about *The Miracle Morning: The Miracle Morning for Entrepreneurs, The Miracle Morning for Writers, The Miracle Morning for Network Marketers, The Miracle Morning for Sales People,* and more.

One of the most successful book series of all time is the *Chicken Soup for the Soul* series, which has hundreds of books under that brand and has made millions of dollars.

This book was rejected by dozens of publishers, including the biggest New York publishing houses, but went on to sell over 112 million copies and were translated into 40 languages. *Chicken Soup for the Soul* also holds the record in *The Guinness Book of World Records* for having the most books on the New York Times bestseller list at one time.

I bet those publishing houses regret not taking on this book when they had the opportunity to do so.

Believe in Yourself Even if Others Don't

If you look back in time, you'll see a lot of "experts" and "authorities" were wrong, especially about books that went on to sell millions of copies.

Here are some examples of popular books that were rejected by the experts and authorities:

- *Chicken Soup for the Soul* – 144 rejections
- *Zen and the Art of Motorcycle Maintenance* – 121 rejections
- *The Help* (became a blockbuster movie) – 60 rejections
- *Carrie* (by Stephen King) – 30 rejections
- *A Time to Kill* (John Grisham) – 28 rejections
- *Dr. Seuss* – 27 rejections
- *Lord of the Flies* – 21 rejections
- *The Diary of Anne Frank* – 15 rejections

The Bible says,

Where there is no vision, the people perish.

You must have a vision for your life and your books. Don't put all your faith and hope in the experts because they are often wrong.

If you want to make a living with your writing, you absolutely can, but just know that it doesn't happen overnight.

We learn by executing, not just by reading and studying. Action is the key to your success.

We're coming to the end of this book, and you have a choice.

You can buy another book and keep reading about writing books and making a living as a writer, or you can start writing your book now. I highly recommend you write a book a month to create deadlines and avoid thinking you have all the time in the world to write a book.

Plan out the books you will write for the entire year. If writing a book a month is too ambitious, then commit to writing a book every quarter. This is doable for everyone.

I just listened to Jenessa Mackenzie's *The Elevated Entrepreneur* podcast interview with bestselling finance author, Rachel Richards, who retired at age 27 with over $10,000 in monthly passive income which comes from three different sources. One of those sources is her two bestselling books:

- *Passive Income, Aggressive Retirement*

- *Money Honey*

Since that episode aired, Rachel's income from her books has increased substantially. At the time of this writing, the eBook version of *Passive Income, Aggressive Retirement,* is making over $37,000 a month!

Is that incredible or what?

I love what Rachel Richards said in the interview,

> *Once you have enough passive income to cover your living expenses, YOU ARE RETIRED.*

Retiring early motivated me to write a book a month!

I wrote about this in detail in my book, *Digital Retirement,* where I talk about draining my 401K because of a financial emergency when the housing market crashed in 2008. My retirement plan vanished overnight so I had to come up with a new one.

I also discovered most people are not prepared for retirement, and I became obsessed with helping others create enough passive income by writing one short book a month so they don't have to struggle financially and can potentially retire early.

Rachel Richards is a millennial, and I am a baby boomer, but we both have the same message.

YOU HAVE THE POWER TO CREATE FINANCIAL INDEPENDENCE RIGHT NOW!

CLOSING THOUGHTS

Remember in the movie *Elf* when Santa's sleigh wouldn't fly because there wasn't enough "Christmas Cheer?" Well, there's a line from the movie that I love:

> *"The best way to spread Christmas Cheer*
> *is singing loud for ALL to hear."*

Once the crowd started singing to express their Christmas Cheer, Santa's sleigh could fly!

It's the same thing with you and your writing. You have to believe in yourself by "singing loud for ALL to hear," and you do that by "writing books for ALL to read."

It starts with action.

Maybe you don't believe it right now, and perhaps you won't believe it when you write your first book, but I promise, if you wrote a book a month for a year, your belief level would skyrocket!

Unfortunately, we are not only fighting against others who don't believe in us, but we are also fighting a battle within ourselves. Don't listen or give credence to the voice inside you that says you can't do it. Take action in spite of that negative voice. I wish I had done this a long time ago.

I'll end with a beautiful quote I heard once,

"The forest would be a very quiet place if only the most talented birds sang."

You have a voice. Go use it and sing your song. If writing is your medium, express yourself that way.

Here's to your Writing Success!

Michelle Kulp

12/28/20, Finishing my 12th book in 12 consecutive months!

Made in United States
Orlando, FL
12 December 2022

26292239R00063